AMERICANA SAMPLER

from Fons and Porter

Americana Sampler

© 2000 by Marianne Fons, Liz Porter, and Oxmoor House
Published by Oxmoor House, Inc., and Leisure Arts, Inc.

Oxmoor House, Inc.
Book Division of Southern Progress Corporation
P.O. Box 2463
Birmingham, Alabama 35201

Library of Congress Catalog Number: 99-85950
ISBN: 0-8487-2360-0
Printed in the United States of America
Third Printing 2001

Editor-in-Chief: Nancy Fitzpatrick Wyatt
Senior Crafts Editor: Susan Ramey Cleveland
Senior Editor, Copy and Homes: Olivia Kindig Wells
Art Director: James Boone

Americana Sampler

Editors: Catherine Corbett Fowler, Lois Martin, Rhonda Richards
Copy Editor: L. Amanda Owens
Editorial Assistant: Suzanne Powell
Associate Art Director: Cynthia R. Cooper
Designer: Melissa Jones Clark
Illustrator: Kelly Davis
Senior Photographer: John O'Hagan
Photo Stylist: Linda Baltzell Wright
Director, Production and Distribution: Phillip Lee
Associate Production Manager: Theresa L. Beste
Production Assistant: Faye Porter Bonner

We're Here for You!

We at Oxmoor House are dedicated to serving you with reliable information that expands your imagination and enriches your life. We welcome your comments and suggestions.

Please write us at:

Oxmoor House
Editor, *Americana Sampler*
2100 Lakeshore Drive
Birmingham, AL 35209

To order additional publications, call 1-800-633-4910.

Contents

You may recognize these blocks *from our book* **Quilter's Complete Guide.** *When we wrote that basic quilting book, we created teaching sequences using traditional patchwork and appliqué blocks. Each time we'd make block units for a photo sequence, we'd make two extra completed blocks—one for each of us. We each kept our blocks in a pizza box. When the book was just about finished, our pizza boxes were full. It was time to sew our blocks into our two sampler quilts.*

Before you start your own sampler, *we suggest you try a trick we did when making our samplers. We put together two identical scrap bags. Every time we made a block, we drew fabrics from our own scrap bag. Compile ½- to 1-yard pieces of approximately 30 different fabrics for your scrap bag. By doing this, your quilt will have color and fabric unity.*

Once your blocks are made, *you can arrange them in a horizontal or vertical orientation (see pages 6 and 7) as we did, or you can come up with your own arrangement.*

Making our sampler quilts was loads of fun. *They are extraspecial friendship quilts that remind us of the fun we had writing* **Quilter's Complete Guide.**

We hope *you enjoy making your quilt, too!*

Liz + Marianne

Americana Sampler

Marianne's Quilt

Horizontal Setting Diagram
Finished Size: 94" x 70"

1. Road to Paradise
2. St Louis
3. Spiral Diamonds
4. Country Angel
5. Grandmother's Fan
6. Windblown Square
7. Royal Cross
8. Ohio Star
9. Spacer: *Cut 2½ " x 8½" strip, made by joining 8 (1½" x 2½") rectangles.*
10. Toad in the Puddle
11. Memory
12. Checkerboard
13. Posy
14. Nine-Patch & Hourglass
15. Nine-Patch
16. Shoo-Fly
17. Sweetheart
18. Four-in-Nine Patch
19. Sawtooth Strip
20. Jacob's Ladder
21. Heart and Hand
22. Bow Tie
23. Celtic True Lover's Knot
24. Big Dipper

25. Wheels
26. Goose Chase Strip
27. Spacer: *Cut 1½" x 12½" strip.*
28. LeMoyne Star
29. Dresden Plate
30. Lone Star
31. Baby Blocks
32. Hole in the Barn Door
33. Checkerboard
34. Broderie Perse Butterfly
35. Sawtooth Star
36. Gentleman's Fancy
37. Rail Fence Strip
38. Rambler
39. Log Cabin
40. Floral Wreath
41. Spiral Diamonds
42. North Carolina Lily
43. Criss-Cross
44. Schoolhouse
45. Goose Chase Strip
46. Cross and Crown
47. Bear's Paw
48. Hawaiian Breadfruit
49. Heart Basket

Quilt Top Assembly Diagram

Block Identifier Diagram

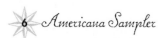

Liz's Quilt

Quilt Top Assembly Diagram

Vertical Setting Diagram
Finished Size: 70" x 94"

Block Identifier Diagram

1. Schoohouse
2. Criss-Cross
3. Goose Chase Strip
4. Spacer: *Cut 1½" x 12½" strip.*
5. LeMoyne Star
6. Dresden Plate
7. Ohio Star
8. Sweetheart
9. Nine-Patch
10. Hole in the Barn Door
11. Four-in-Nine Patch
12. Nine-Patch & Hourglass
13. Cross and Crown
14. Log Cabin
15. Lone Star
16. Sawtooth Strip
17. Heart and Hand

18. Shoo-Fly
19. Grandmother's Fan
20. Royal Cross
21. Rail Fence Strip
22. Bear's Paw
23. Celtic True Lover's Knot
24. Bow Tie
25. Windblown Square
26. Rambler
27. Floral Wreath
28. Hawaiian Breadfruit
29. Jacob's Ladder
30. Rail Fence Strip
31. Posy
32. Baby Blocks
33. Big Dipper
34. Checkerboard

35. Broderie Perse Butterfly
36. Toad in the Puddle
37. Sawtooth Strip
38. Memory
39. Spiral Diamonds
40. Heart Basket
41. North Carolina Lily

42. Gentleman's Fancy
43. Goose Chase Strip
44. Sawtooth Star
45. Wheels
46. Country Angel
47. Road to Paradise
48. St. Louis
49. Hourglass Strip

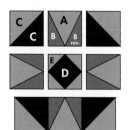
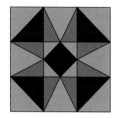

Block Assembly Diagram   *Block Diagram*

Finished Size: 9" square

Materials
Scraps of red, teal, and tan fabrics
Template plastic

Cutting
Make templates for patterns A and B. (See page 41 for pattern.)

From red fabric, cut:
- 1 (3½") D square.
- 2 (3⅞") squares. Cut each square in half diagonally to make total of 4 C triangles.

From teal fabric, cut:
- 4 B triangles and 4 B reverse triangles.

From tan fabric, cut:
- 2 (3⅞") squares. Cut each square in half diagonally to make 4 C triangles.
- 4 A triangles.
- 4 (2") squares to make E triangles.

Assembly
1. Stitch 1 red C triangle to 1 tan C triangle to make triangle-square. Repeat to make total of 4 red/tan triangle-squares.

2. Stitch 1 teal B triangle and 1 teal B reverse triangle to long sides of tan A triangle to make square. Repeat to make total of 4 squares.

3. Use diagonal-seams method (see page 21) to stitch 1 tan E square to each corner of red D square to make block center.

4. Referring to *Block Assembly Diagram*, join units into 3 horizontal rows and then join rows to complete block.

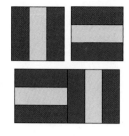

Block Assembly Diagram   *Block Diagram*

Finished Size: 9" square

Materials
Scraps of blue, white, and brown fabrics

Cutting
- Cut 1 (2"-wide) strip from each of 3 fabrics. With each length of fabric, fold into fourths and place ruler atop folded fabric so that it measures desired strip width. Cut through all layers, guiding cutter along edge of ruler (Photo A).

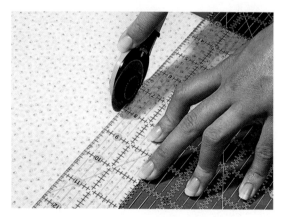

Photo A

Assembly
1. To make strip set, with right sides facing and raw edges aligned, pair 2 different strips. Machine-stitch with ¼" seam along long edge (Photo B). Add third strip to complete strip set.

Photo B

2. Press seams of strip set. Begin by pressing strips flat, just as you have sewn them, to set stitching (Photo C).

Photo C

3. Fold top fabric strip back, revealing right side of strip set. Gently, with side of iron, press seam on right side, with seam allowances to 1 side (Photo D). Press with up-and-down motion instead of sliding iron so that you do not stretch fabric.

Photo D

4. Align horizontal mark on ruler with long edge of strip set. Cut along ruler edge, trimming uneven end of strip set (Photo E).

Photo E

5. Turn strip set around so that trimmed end of strip set is near left edge of mat. Keeping horizontal line on ruler aligned with long edge of strip set, measure 5". Cut 5" square along ruler edge (Photo F). Cut total of 4 (5") squares from strip set.

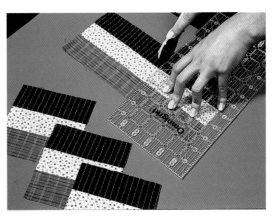

Photo F

6. Lay out units to form block, with blue or brown edges at center as desired. Join 2 units for top half of block. Repeat for bottom half. Join halves to complete block.

Country Angel

Block Assembly Diagram

Block Diagram

Finished Size: 18" square

Materials

½ yard beige print for background square
½ yard medium blue check for setting triangles
Scraps blue print for dress and sleeves
Scraps light blue print for wings
Scraps brown, gold, or black print for hair
Muslin scraps for face and hands
Scrap black print for shoes
¼ yard medium/dark plaid for inner border
Rotary cutter, cutting mat, and acrylic ruler
Fine-point permanent brown fabric marker
Cotton swab
Powdered blush
Template plastic
Pencil
Fabric glue stick
Spray water bottle
Tweezers

Making Patterns

Trace patterns on page 42 onto template plastic. Make finished-size template for each piece, such as angel's face. When making templates for pieces that are overlapped by others, use dashed lines on pattern as seam-line guides. Mark wing and shoe placement lines on dress template. Mark appropriate pieces for left and right (as for wings and dress sleeves).

Cutting

Cutting instructions for squares and triangles include ¼" seam allowances. Add ³⁄₁₆" seam allowances to all sides when cutting appliqué pieces.

From beige print, cut:
• 1 (11½") background square.

From medium blue check, cut:
• 2 (11") squares. Cut each square in half diagonally to make total of 4 setting triangles. Triangles will be oversize; you will trim finished block to size later.

From blue print, cut:
• 1 dress, 1 right sleeve, and 1 left sleeve.

From light blue print, cut:
• 1 right wing and 1 left wing.

From brown, gold, or black print, cut:
• 1 hair.

From muslin, cut:
• 1 face, 1 right hand, and 1 left hand.

From black print, cut:
• 1 right shoe and 1 left shoe.

From medium/dark plaid, cut:
• 2 (1¼" x 11½") strips for inner border.
• 2 (1¼" x 13") strips for inner border.

Assembly

Many appliqué pieces overlap, such as with the angel's dress and wings. When preparing overlapping appliqué pieces, don't turn under any seam allowance that will be covered by another piece. And remember, always work from the background to the foreground.

—Marianne

1. Using marker, trace eyes and mouth on face. Use cotton swab to apply small amount of powdered blush to angel's cheeks.

2. Prepare appliqué pieces by turning under raw edges.

3. Fold background square in half diagonally and lightly press to form placement line. Fold dress in half lengthwise; lightly crease to form guideline. Align dress guideline with fold in background square. Position dress hem about 3½" from bottom raw corner of square. Pin dress in place.

4. Using placement lines as guides, slide shoes and wings under dress. Appliqué shoes and wings to background square and then appliqué dress. When stitching pieces that are underneath others, fold back overlapping pieces and pin out of way.

To trim background fabric from behind appliqués, turn work to wrong side, pinch fabrics to separate layers, and make small cut in background fabric. Cut background fabric within appliquéd area, leaving ¼" seam allowance.

—Liz

5. Pin sleeves in place and tuck hands under sleeves. Appliqué hands and then sleeves; appliqué face and then hair. Trim background fabric from behind pieces.

6. Stitch 11½"-long plaid strips to opposite sides of background square; then stitch 13"-long plaid strips to remaining 2 sides.

7. Stitch 1 setting triangle to opposite sides of angel block. Stitch remaining setting triangles to remaining sides of block.

8. Use rotary cutter and ruler to trim block to 18½" square (including seam allowances).

Grandmother's Fan

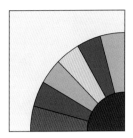

Block Diagram

Finished Size: 12" square

Materials
6 (3½" x 7") pastel prints for blades
1 (4¾") square dark print for handle
1 (12½") square tan fabric
Template plastic

Cutting
Make templates for patterns A and B. (See page 41 for patterns.)

From each pastel print, cut:
• 1 fan blade (A).

From dark print, cut:
• 1 fan handle (B).

Assembly
1. Join fan blades in an arc.

2. Fold under outer curved edge of fan arc and curve of handle piece; baste.

3. Position handle at one corner of background square. Position arc at corners tucking lower edge of arc under curved edge of handle. Pin pieces in place. Appliqué arc and handle to background square.

4. Carefully trim tan fabric from under arc and handle. Press.

Windblown Square

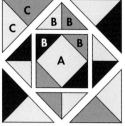

Block Assembly Diagram    Block Diagram

Finished Size: 12" square

Materials
Scraps red, gold, and light prints

Cutting
From gold print, cut:
- 1 (7¼") square. Cut in quarters diagonally to make 4 C triangles. (You will have 2 extra.)
- 2 (3⅞") squares. Cut in half diagonally to make 4 B triangles.

From red print, cut:
- 1 (7¼") square. Cut in quarters diagonally to make 4 C triangles. (You will have 2 extra.)
- 2 (3⅞") squares. Cut in half diagonally to make 4 B triangles.

From light print, cut:
- 1 (4¾") square (A).
- 1 (7¼") square. Cut in quarters diagonally to make 4 C triangles.
- 2 (3⅞") squares. Cut in half diagonally to make 4 B triangles.

Assembly
1. Join 2 red B triangles and 2 gold B triangles to A square (Diagram 1).
2. Make 2 gold/light triangle B units, as shown in Diagram 2, and 2 red/light triangle B units.

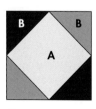

Diagram 2

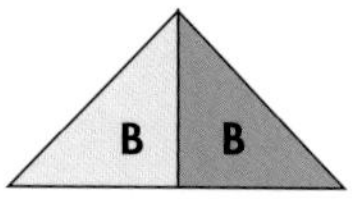

Diagram 1

3. Make 2 red/light triangle C units, as shown in Diagram 3, and 2 gold/light triangle C units.
4. Referring to Block Assembly Diagram, join B triangle units to A unit; then join C triangle units to sides.

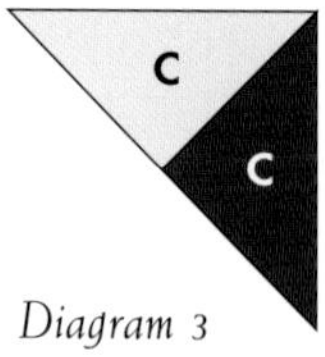

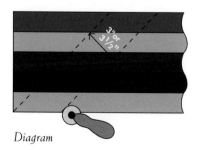

Diagram 3

✳ ✳ ✳ ✳ ✳ ✳ ✳ ✳

Spiral Diamonds

Strip Diagram

Finished Sizes:
1 (2½" x 25") strip
1 (3" x 34") strip

Materials
2½"-wide crosswise strips of 5 different fabrics
Rotary cutter, mat, and ruler with 45°-angle marking

Assembly
1. Join 5 strips lengthwise to make strip set. Press seam allowances to 1 side.
2. Trim end of strip set at 45°-angle. Cut 3"-wide segments and 3½"-wide segments (see Diagram).
3. Join 3" strips as shown in Strip Diagram to make 25½" length. Join 3½" strips as shown in Strip Diagram to make 34½" length.

Diagram

Royal Cross

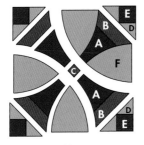

Block Assembly Diagram

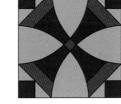

Block Diagram

Finished Size: 12" square

Materials
Scraps red, gold, and tan prints
Template plastic

Making Patterns
Make templates for pattern pieces A, B, and F (on page 43), including registration marks (indicated by Xs). Use a large needle to make holes in template seam allowances at registration marks; mark through holes onto fabric.

Cutting
From red print, cut:
- 4 As, using template.
- 4 (2⅜") squares (E).

From gold print, cut:
- 4 Bs, using template.
- 1 (1½") square (C).

From tan print, cut:
- 4 (2¾") squares. Cut each square in half diagonally to make 8 Ds.
- 4 Fs, using template.

Assembly
1. Referring to *Block Assembly Diagram*, join 1 A and 1 B. Repeat to make total of 4 A/B units. Join 2 A/B units to 2 sides of C to make center unit.
2. Match curved side of 1 F to curved side of 1 A/B unit, aligning registration marks. Pin in place and stitch. Join another F to opposite side of A/B unit. Repeat to make total of 2 A/B/F units. Join A/B/F units to center unit.
3. Join 2 Ds and 1 E as shown in *Block Assembly*

Diagram. Repeat to make total of 4 D/E units. Add 1 D/E unit to each corner.

✳ ✳ ✳ ✳ ✳ ✳ ✳ ✳ ✳

Ohio Star

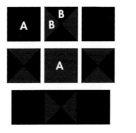

Block Assembly Diagram

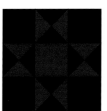

Block Diagram

Finished Size: 12" square

Materials
Scraps red and black prints

Cutting
From red print, cut:
- 1 (4½") square (A).
- 2 (5¼") squares. Cut squares in quarters diagonally to make 8 triangles (B).

From black print, cut:
- 4 (4½") squares (A).
- 2 (5¼") squares. Cut squares in quarters diagonally to make 8 triangles (B).

Assembly
1. Join 1 red B and 1 black B to make 1 pieced unit as shown in *Quarter-Square Triangle Assembly Diagram.* Make 8 units. Join 2 units along long sides to make square. Make total of 4 pieced B squares.

Quarter-Square Triangle Assembly Diagram

2. Lay out A squares and pieced B squares as shown in *Block Assembly Diagram*. Join into rows; join rows to complete block.

Toad in the Puddle

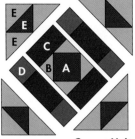

Corner Unit

Block Assembly Diagram   *Block Diagram*

Finished Size: 8" square

Materials

Scraps of gray, dark blue, medium blue, and red fabrics

Cutting

From gray fabric, cut:
- 6 (2⅞") squares. Cut each square in half diagonally to make 12 E triangles.
- 4 (2") squares to make B triangles.

From dark blue fabric, cut:
- 2 (2⅞") squares. Cut each square in half diagonally to make 4 E triangles.
- 1 (3⅜") A square.

From medium blue fabric, cut:
- 4 (1⅞") D squares.

From red fabric, cut:
- 4 (1⅞" x 3⅜") C rectangles.

Assembly

1. Use diagonal-seams method (see page 21) to join 1 gray B square to each corner of dark blue A square to make center square.

2. Stitch red C rectangles to 2 opposite sides of center square. Add medium blue D squares to remaining red C rectangles and stitch these to remaining 2 sides of center square.

3. Make triangle-square by joining 1 dark blue E triangle to 1 gray E triangle. Repeat to make total of 4 blue/gray triangle-squares.

4. Make Corner Unit by stitching 2 gray E triangles to adjacent blue sides of 1 triangle-square. Repeat to make total of 4 Corner Units.

5. Stitch 2 Corner Units to opposite sides of block center. Complete block by adding remaining Corner Units.

Memory

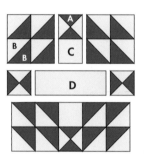

Block Assembly Diagram

Block Diagram

Finished Size: 10" square

Materials

Scraps of blue and white-on-white prints

Cutting

From blue print, cut:
- 2 (3¼") squares. Cut squares in quarters diagonally to make 8 As.
- 8 (2⅞") squares. Cut squares in half diagonally to make 16 Bs.

From white-on-white print, cut:
- 2 (3¼") squares. Cut squares in quarters diagonally to make 8 As.
- 8 (2⅞") squares. Cut squares in half diagonally to make 16 Bs.
- 2 (2½") squares (C).
- 1 (2½" x 6½") rectangle (D).

Assembly

1. Join 2 blue As and 2 white As to make 1 pieced square *(Diagram 1)*. Repeat to make total of 4 units.
2. Join 1 blue B and 1 white B along long sides to make triangle-square. Repeat to make total of 16 triangle-squares. Join 4 triangle-squares to make 1 B unit *(Diagram 2)*. Repeat to make 4 units.

Diagram 1

Diagram 2

3. Referring to *Block Assembly Diagram*, join 1 A unit to 1 C as shown. Repeat to make total of 2 units. Join 2 B units to 1 A/C unit for top row. Repeat with remaining B and A/C units for bottom row.
4. Join 1 A unit to each end of D for middle row. Join rows to complete block. Press.

This traditional block was often used in the 1900s for friendship quilts. The maker penned her name in the center rectangle and then traded her block with quilting friends.

—Marianne

✳ ✳ ✳ ✳ ✳ ✳ ✳ ✳ ✳

Checkerboard

Block Assembly Diagram

Block Diagram

Finished Size: 4" x 6" block

Materials

1 (1½" x 22") cream strip
1 (1½" x 22") red strip

Assembly

1. Join 1½"-wide strips lengthwise to form strip set.
2. Cut 12 (1½"-wide) segments from strip set. Join segments, reversing positions of segments so that contrasting fabrics alternate in checkerboard fashion.

Posy

Block Diagram

Finished Size: 6" square

Materials

1 (6½") square tan print
Scraps of green, yellow, and pink prints
Template plastic

Cutting

Make templates for pattern pieces. (See page 44 for patterns.) Add ³⁄₁₆" seam allowances when cutting appliqué pieces.

From green print, cut:
- 1 (1" x 5") bias strip for stem.
- 2 green leaves (A).

From yellow print, cut:
- 1 center (C).

From pink print, cut:
- 1 posy (B).

Assembly

1. Fold bias strip in half lengthwise with wrong sides facing; press. Fold in half lengthwise again, placing raw edges just inside folded edge. Press.

2. Referring to *Block Diagram* on page 15 and aligning folded strip so that the raw edges are along 1 side of stem position, stitch bias stem onto tan background (Photo A). Use a running stitch to stitch along inside crease of first fold. Bring folded edge over to cover raw edges and appliqué in place (Photo B).

3. Appliqué leaves (A), posy (B), and posy center (C) in place.

Photo A

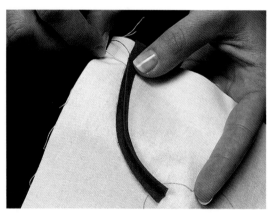

Photo B

Nine-Patch & Hourglass

Nine-Patch Diagrams

Hourglass Diagrams

Block Diagram

Finished Size: 18" x 27" block

Materials
¼ yard each of 6 assorted fabrics (5 dark and 1 light)
¼ yard brown print
¼ yard cream print

Cutting
From assorted dark fabrics, cut:
• 5 (2"-wide) strips.
From light fabric, cut:
• 4 (2"-wide) strips.
From brown print, cut:
• Cut 1 (5¾"-wide) strip. Cut strip into 6 (5¾") squares for Hourglass Block.
From cream print, cut:
• Cut 1 (5¾"-wide) strip. Cut strip into 6 (5¾") squares for Hourglass Block.

Assembly

1. To make Nine-Patch Block, stitch 3 strip sets, alternating strip placement to match row in finished block (See photo). Press seams toward dark strips.

Photo

2. Cut across seam lines of each strip set at 2" intervals to form segments. (To pair rows, before cutting, stack strip set for first row on top of strip set for second row, with right sides facing.) Cut 24 segments with dark ends and 12 segments with dark centers.

3. Arrange segments into rows. Join rows to complete block. Make 12 Nine-Patch Blocks.

4. To make Hourglass Blocks, place 1 (5¾") cream print square on top of 1 (5¾") brown print square, with right sides facing. Draw diagonal line from corner to corner on top square. Stitch exactly ¼" on each side of drawn line (*Diagram 1*). Cut along drawn line to make 2 triangle-square units (*Diagram 2*). Press seam allowances toward dark fabric. You will have 2 completed triangle squares (*Diagram 3*).

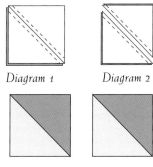

Diagram 1   *Diagram 2*

Diagram 3

5. Pair triangle-square units, with right sides facing, contrasting fabric triangles together, and seams aligned. Draw diagonal line from corner to corner. Stitch ¼" along each side of drawn line (*Diagram 4*). Cut along drawn line to separate units (*Diagram 5*). You will have 2 units. Press completed Hourglass Blocks (*Diagram 6*).

6. Repeat Steps 4 and 5 to make total of 12 Hourglass Blocks. Refer to *Block Diagram* on page 16 and join Hourglass Blocks with Nine-Patch Blocks to complete unit.

Diagram 4   *Diagram 5*   *Diagram 6*

Nine Patch

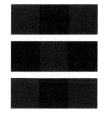   

Block Assembly Diagram   *Block Diagram*

Finished Size: 9" square

Materials

5 (3½") squares red print
4 (3½") squares blue print

Assembly

Join squares as shown in *Block Assembly Diagram* to make 1 Nine-Patch Block.

Shoo-Fly

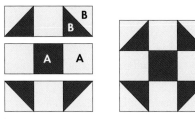

Block Assembly Diagram   Block Diagram

Finished Size: 9" square

Materials
Scraps of blue plaid and light print

Cutting

From blue plaid, cut:
- 1 (3½") square (A).
- 2 (3⅞") squares. Cut squares in half diagonally to make 4 triangles (B).

From light print, cut:
- 4 (3½") squares (A).
- 2 (3⅞") squares. Cut squares in half diagonally to make 4 triangles (B).

Assembly
1. Join 1 blue plaid B and 1 light B to make square. Repeat to make total of 4 squares.
2. Arrange As and pieced squares as shown in *Block Assembly Diagram*. Join into rows; join rows to complete block.

Sweetheart

Block Assembly Diagram

Finished Size: 9" square

Materials
9½" square background fabric
Scraps of 4 different fabrics for hearts
Thread in colors to match heart fabrics
Freezer paper or tracing paper
Pencil
Fabric glue stick
Spray water bottle
Tweezers

Cutting

When cutting the heart appliqué pieces, place the freezer-paper templates on the fabric at an angle so that—as much as possible—the outer edges of the shape will be on the bias, thus reducing fraying.

—Liz

Making Patterns
Trace heart pattern (see page 48) 4 times onto uncoated (dull) side of freezer paper.

Cutting

From each heart fabric:
- Using dry iron at wool setting, press shiny side of 1 freezer-paper pattern to wrong side of each fabric. Cut out, adding ³⁄₁₆" seam allowance.

Assembly
1. Fold background square in half vertically, horizontally, and diagonally both ways. Finger-press to make guidelines.
2. On each heart, use small sharp scissors to clip into seam allowances at cleft of heart.
3. Apply fabric glue to wrong side of seam allowances. Use your fingers to fold seam allowances over edges to paper side of template; glue in place. When folding under points, such as at bottom of heart, fold point back first (*Folding Diagrams, Figure 1*), then seam allowance on 1 side (*Figure 2*), and seam allowance on adjacent side of point (*Figure 3*).
4. Referring to *Block Assembly Diagram*, pin prepared appliqués in place on background square. Position hearts along diagonal guidelines, with cleft 2¾" from center.

Figure 1   *Figure 2*   *Figure 3*

Folding Diagrams

5. Hand- or machine-appliqué hearts in place, using matching regular sewing or embroidery thread.

6. After stitching, turn block to wrong side. Cut background fabric from behind appliqués, leaving ¼" seam allowances. Moisten fabric with spray of water to dissolve glue; use tweezers to remove paper pieces.

Four-in-Nine Patch

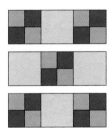 

Block Assembly Diagram   *Block Diagram*

Finished Size: 9" square

Materials

⅛ yard each of 3 fabrics (2 dark or medium, 1 light)
Rotary cutter, mat, and ruler

Cutting

• Cut 1 (2"-wide) strip from each dark or medium fabric.

• Cut 1 (3½"-wide) strip from light fabric. Cut strip into 4 (3½") squares (Photo A).

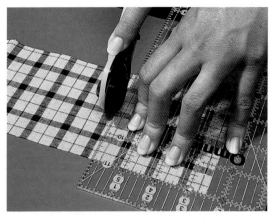

Photo A

Assembly

1. Join 2"-wide strips lengthwise to form strip set. Press seam allowances to 1 side.

2. Cut strip sets into 2 (21") long pieces. Pair strip sets with right sides facing. Cut 5 (2"-wide) segments from paired strip sets (10 segments total) as shown in Photo B. Chain-piece paired segments (Photo C).

Photo B

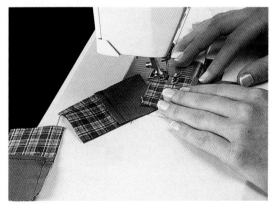

Photo C

3. Lay out 5 Four-Patch Units and 4 light squares as shown in Photo D. Join units into 3 rows with 3 units in each row; join rows to complete block.

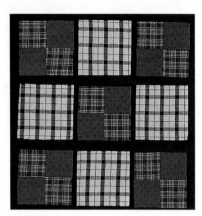

Photo D

Note: *Cut 4 extra segments and join in checkerboard fashion to make 1 (3" x 6") unit. Set aside. (You will use this Checkerboard strip later when assembling the quilt top. See Horizontal Setting Diagram, Block 33 on page 6 and Vertical Setting Digram, Block 34 on page 7.)*

Your sewing machine will almost automatically match seams for you if you arrange pairs so that seam allowances on the top segment point away from you and seam allowances on the bottom segment point toward you as you sew.

—Marianne

Jacob's Ladder

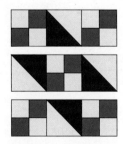 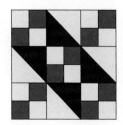

Block Assembly Diagram   *Block Diagram*

Finished Size: 9" square

Materials

Scrap of red print
Fat eighth cream print
Fat eighth blue print

Cutting

From red print and cream print, cut:

• 2 (3⅞") squares each. Cut each square in half diagonally to make 4 half-square triangles of each color.

From blue print and cream print, cut:

• 1 (2" x 22") strip each.

Assembly

1. Join 1 cream and 1 red triangle to make triangle-square. Repeat to make total of 4 triangle-squares.

2. Join blue and cream strips lengthwise to make strip set. Press seam allowances to 1 side.

3. Cut 10 (2"-wide) segments from strip set. Join segments in pairs, reversing positions of segments so that contrasting fabrics alternate in checkerboard fashion, for a total of 5 Four-Patch Units. Join units as shown in *Block Assembly Diagram*.

Heart and Hand

Block Diagram

Finished Size: 9" square

Materials

1 (9½") square dark brown or tan print for background
1 (9") square light brown or red print for hand

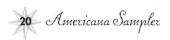

1 (3") square yellow or black print for heart
Thread to match hand fabric
Freezer paper

Assembly

1. Trace hand and heart patterns on page 48 separately onto smooth side of freezer paper.
2. Cut out freezer-paper hand pattern. Press shiny side of paper to right side of hand fabric. Use pencil to mark along edge of paper, marking fold over line. Cut out fabric hand, adding ⅛" seam allowance.
3. Remove freezer paper. Clip seam allowances on inside curves, taking care not to clip past drawn line.
4. Pin hand to background square. Appliqué, turning under seam allowance with your needle as you stitch.
5. Press paper heart onto right side of palm of appliquéd hand. Draw line along edge of paper. Remove paper. Cut out heart in hand, adding ⅛" seam allowance to inside of heart.
6. Insert 3" square underlay in opening, right side up, and baste or pin in place.
7. Use needle-turn appliqué to turn under and to appliqué heart opening to reveal underlay.

Bow Tie

Block Assembly Diagram   *Block Diagram*

Finished Size: 4 (6") squares

Materials

Scraps of 4 different fabrics
8 (3½") squares cream fabric

Cutting

From each scrap fabric, cut:
- 2 (3½") squares.
- 2 (2") squares.

Assembly

1. Use diagonal-seams method (see below) to stitch 1 (2") square of first scrap fabric to 1 corner of 1 cream square. Repeat to make total of 2 units.
2. Arrange units with 2 (3½") squares of same scrap fabric to make 2 horizontal rows (*Block Assembly Diagram*). Join units in each row; then join rows to complete block. Repeat to make total of 4 Bow Tie Blocks.

Stitching Diagonal Seams

This quick-piecing technique requires a little more fabric than traditional triangle piecing but compensates with lots of ease and speed.

Start with base fabric square or rectangle (project instructions tell you size to cut both pieces). Contrasting corner always starts out as square. Finger-press contrasting corner on diagonal to make seam guide.

1. With right sides facing, match small square to 1 corner of base fabric. Stitch from corner to corner through both layers, being careful to sew straight seam (Photo A).

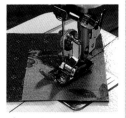

Photo A

2. Press small square in half at seam and trim excess fabric behind stitched corner, leaving ¼" seam allowance (Photo B).

Photo B

3. If desired, repeat Steps 1 and 2 to add diagonal corner to 2, 3, or all 4 corners of base square or rectangle.

Celtic True Lover's Knot

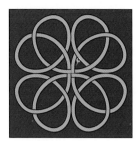

Block Diagram

Finished Size: 12" square

Materials

1 (12½") square red solid for background
½ yard black-and-white check for appliqué
⅜"-wide bias pressing bar
Tracing paper
Fine-tip permanent black marker
Water-soluble dressmaker's pen

Assembly

Note: *Bias pressing bars, made of metal or heat-resistant plastic, make preparing lengths of consistent-width folded bias strips easy. You can buy these bars, usually in sets of 3 widths, at quilt shops and from mail-order suppliers. Package instructions tell you how wide to cut fabric strip for each bar.*

1. To make master pattern, fold 12½" square of tracing paper in half vertically and horizontally, creasing to make guidelines. Unfold paper and trace quarter pattern on page 45 onto 1 quadrant, aligning broken lines on pattern with fold lines on paper. Rotate paper and trace design in remaining quadrants to make complete pattern. Trace placement lines with black marker.

2. Center and pin background square on top of paper pattern. Working at window or light table, lightly trace placement lines onto fabric with dressmaker's pen.

If you don't have a light table and want to work at night, make a quick temporary light table by placing a lamp underneath a glass-topped table.

—Liz

3. Cut 1⅛"-wide bias strips from appliqué fabric. With wrong sides facing, fold each strip in half lengthwise and machine-stitch ⅛" from long raw edge.

4. Insert ⅜"-wide bias bar into 1 sewn strip. Adjust strip so that seam is centered on 1 side of bar. Press seam flat. Turn bar over and press other side. Slide bar through strip until entire strip is pressed. (Be careful: Metal bar gets hot!) Repeat for each strip.

5. With seam side down, baste bias strips in place within marked placement lines, placing strips in same over/under configuration as shown on pattern (see photo). Start new strip at place where another strip will cover raw end.

6. Appliqué both sides of strips. On each section of design, stitch inner curves first and then outer curves.

Photo

Big Dipper

Finished Size: 12" square

Materials

2 (7¼") squares cream print
8 (7¼") squares assorted dark prints
Note: *If piecing quilt top in Vertical Setting, also cut 7 (4¼") cream squares and 7 (4¼") assorted dark squares. (See Block 49 of Vertical Setting Diagram on page 7.)*

Cutting

Cut 4 triangles from each square by cutting each square in quarters diagonally to make 4 quarter-square triangles.

Assembly

1. Using *Block Assembly Diagram* as guide, join 4 triangles into a square unit. Make 4 square units. Join units as shown to complete Big Dipper. You will have 24 dark triangles left over.

2. For Vertical Setting, join 4 smaller triangles into squares. Make 14 squares. Join units in strip as shown in *Vertical Setting Diagram, Block 49* on page 7.

Wheels

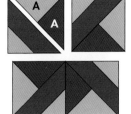

Block Assembly Diagram   Block Diagram

Finished Size: 12" square

Materials

Scraps of brown, blue, and red prints

Cutting

From brown print, cut:
- 1 (7¼") square. Cut into quarters diagonally for 4 As.
- 4 (3½") squares.

From blue print, cut:
- 1 (7¼") square. Cut into quarters diagonally for 4 As.

From red print, cut:
- 2 (6⅞") squares. Cut in half diagonally to make 4 triangles.

Assembly

1. Join 1 brown A and 1 blue A to make a large triangle.

2. Use diagonal-seams method (see page 21) and refer to *Diagram* below to add 3½" brown square to red triangle.

3. Join triangles to make quarter-block. Repeat to make total of 4 quarter-blocks.

Diagram

4. Join quarter-blocks, rotating as shown, to complete block.

LeMoyne Star

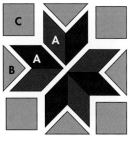

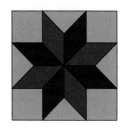

Block Assembly Diagram   Block Diagram

Finished Size: 12" square

Materials

Scraps of red plaid, blue print, and light print
Template plastic

Cutting

Make template for pattern A. See page 44 for pattern. Use a large needle to poke holes in template at corner dots. Mark fabric pieces through holes in template.

From red plaid, cut:

• 4 A diamonds, using template.

From blue print, cut:

• 4 A diamonds, using template.

From light print, cut:

• 1 (6¼") square. Cut in quarters diagonally to make 4 triangles (B).

• 4 (4") squares (C).

Assembly

1. Join 1 red plaid and 1 blue print diamond along 1 edge. Start and end stitching ¼" from ends to leave seam allowances free so that you can set triangles and squares into star. Repeat to make total of 4 units.

2. Join 2 pairs to make half star. Repeat. Join halves to complete star.

3. Set triangles B into alternate openings around star (*Block Assembly Diagram*). Set squares C into remaining openings (see Sewing Set-In Seams above).

Sewing Set-In Seams

1. From outside edge, stitch into corner, stopping at corner seam line. Backstitch at corner to strengthen corner seam. (*Diagram 1*).

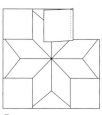

Diagram 1

2. Align remaining sides and sew seam from corner to outside edge (*Diagram 2*).

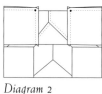

Diagram 2

Dresden Plate

Block Diagram

Finished Size: 12" square

Materials

1 (12½") square rust print
Scraps of red, teal, and brown prints
Template plastic

Cutting

Make template for wedge. See page 44 for pattern.

From scraps, cut:

• 16 wedges.

Assembly

1. Join wedges along straight edges, stitching between indicated points, to form plate.

2. Fold rust square in half vertically and horizontally; finger-press to find center. Unfold.

3. Center plate on square. Turn under ¼" on inside and outside raw edges and appliqué to complete block.

Baby Blocks

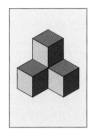

Block Assembly Diagram   *Block Diagram*

Finished Size: 10" x 15" block

Materials
9 scraps of assorted fabrics (3 dark, 3 medium, and 3 light)
1 (10½" x 15½") rectangle blue-and-white stripe fabric for background
Template plastic

Cutting
Make template. See page 45 for pattern. Use a large needle to poke holes in template at corner dots. Mark fabric pieces through holes in template.

From squares, cut:
• 9 Baby Block diamonds.

Assembly
1. Join 1 each of light, medium, and dark diamonds to make a hexagon, matching at corner dots. Repeat to make total of 3 hexagons.

2. Join 3 hexagons as shown. Appliqué to center of background block.

Broderie Perse Butterfly

Broderie Perse Block

Finished Size: 6" square

Materials
Scrap of print with butterfly for appliqué
1 (6½") square light print for background
Embroidery floss

Cutting
Cut out butterfly ⅛" outside edge of design. Cut away small details, such as antennae or tendrils; these can be embroidered later.

Assembly
Center motif on background fabric. Appliqué in place. Embroider details as desired.

Broderie perse is an appliqué technique in which a printed motif, such as a butterfly, a bird, or a flower, is cut from a printed fabric and appliquéd to a background. For this block, choose any printed motif that will fit on your 6½" background square.

—Liz

Lone Star

Block Assembly Diagram

Block Diagram

Finished Size: 28" square

Materials
¼ yard blue print
¼ yard blue check
¼ yard red print
¼ yard tan print
¼ yard black print
½ yard cream print
Ruler with 45° angle line

Cutting
From blue print, cut:
• 1 (2½"-wide) strip.
From blue check, cut:
• 2 (2½"-wide) strips.
From red print, cut:
• 3 (2½"-wide) strips.

From tan print, cut:
• 2 (2½"-wide) strips.
From black print, cut:
• 1 (2½"-wide) strip.
From cream print, cut:
• 1 (8¾"-wide) strip. Cut into 4 (8¾") squares (A).
• 1 (13") square. Cut in quarters diagonally to make 4 B triangles.

Assembly
1. Referring to *Diagram 1*, join 1 strip each of blue print, blue check, and red print in order, staggering each strip approximately 2½" for Row A. Using 45° markings on your ruler, cut across staggered end to make 45° angle. Cut 1 (2½"-wide) strip at 45° angle. After every second or third cut, check to see that angle is still 45° and correct by trimming if necessary. Repeat to cut total of 8 segments.

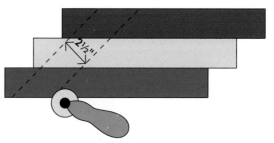

Diagram 1

2. For Row B, make strip set with blue check, red print, and tan print. For Row C, make strip set with red print, tan print, and black print. Cut 8 (2½"-wide) segments from each strip set.
3. Join 1 strip from Row A set with 1 strip from Row B set, matching seams ¼" from fabric edge. Add 1 strip from Row C in same manner to complete 1 large diamond of Lone Star. Repeat to make total of 8 large diamonds.
4. Join 2 segments to make quarter-star unit. Start and end stitching ¼" from ends to leave seam allowances free so that you can set triangles and squares into star. Repeat to make total of 4 units. Join 4 units to complete center of Lone Star. Press seams clockwise.
5. Set in B triangles and A squares to complete block. See page 24 for how to sew set-in seams.

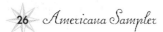

Chart It Out

The simplest way to quick-piece a Lone Star Block is to determine the number of fabrics to be used and then to make a chart and a diagram. This block uses 5 fabrics. Beginning at the center, number the fabrics and then label the rows (*Diagram 2*).

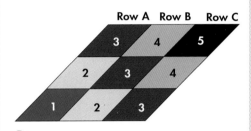

Diagram 2

Make a chart that lists the fabrics and the number of times each appears in the star segment (see below). That is the number of strips to cut from each fabric. Be careful not to stretch the strips at each step, since you will be working with bias edges on 2 sides of the diamonds.

Lone Star Color Chart

Fabric	Color	Cut
I	blue print	I
2	blue check	2
3	red print	3
4	tan print	2
5	black print	I

Hole in the Barn Door

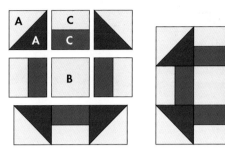

Block Assembly Diagram   *Block Diagram*

Finished Size: 9" square

Materials
Scraps red, blue, and white star prints

Cutting
From red print, cut:
- 2 (3⅞") squares. Cut in half diagonally to make 4 A triangles.

From blue print, cut:
- 4 (2" x 3½") rectangles (C).

From white star print, cut:
- 2 (3⅞") squares. Cut in half diagonally to make 4 A triangles.
- 4 (2" x 3½") rectangles (C).
- 1 (3½") square (B).

Assembly
1. Join 1 red triangle A and 1 white triangle A along long edges to make a square. Repeat to make total of 4 squares.

2. Join 1 white rectangle C and 1 blue rectangle C along long edges to make a square. Repeat to make total of 4 squares.

3. Referring to *Block Assembly Diagram*, join 2 A units to 1 C unit. Repeat. Join 1 C unit to each side of square B. Join rows to complete block.

Sawtooth Star

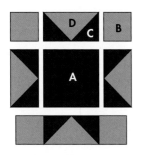

Block Assembly Diagram   *Block Diagram*

Finished Size: 12" square

Materials
Scraps of blue and gold prints

Cutting
From blue print, cut:
- 1 (6½") square (A).
- 4 (3⅞") squares. Cut squares in half diagonally to make 8 triangles (C).

From gold print, cut:
- 4 (3½") squares (B).
- 1 (7¼") square. Cut square in quarters diagonally to make 4 triangles (D).

Assembly
1. Join 1 C to 1 side of 1 D. Join 1 C to other side of D, forming a rectangle. Repeat to make total of 4 units.

2. Join 1 B to 1 end of 1 C/D unit. Join 1 B to opposite end of C/D unit as shown. Repeat to make total of 2 strips.

3. Arrange A and pieced units as shown in *Block Assembly Diagram.* Join into rows; then join rows to complete block.

Gentleman's Fancy

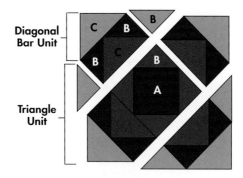

Block Assembly Diagram

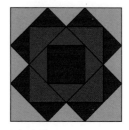

Block Diagram

Finished Size: 12" square

Materials
Scraps of red, teal, brown, and cream prints

Cutting
From red print, cut:
- 1 (6¼") A square.
- 8 (3⅜") squares to make B triangles.

From teal or cream print, cut:
- 4 (3⅜") squares to make B triangles.

From brown print, cut:
- 4 (3⅜" x 6¼") rectangles to make C triangles.

From cream print, cut:
- 2 (4⅞") squares. Cut squares in half diagonally to make total of 4 C triangles.
- 1 (5¼") square. Cut square in quarters diagonally to make total of 4 B triangles.

Assembly
1. Using diagonal-seams method (see page 21), stitch 3⅜" teal or cream squares to opposite corners of red A square. Stitch remaining 2 teal or cream squares to remaining corners to make

center A/B unit.

2. Use diagonal-seams method to stitch 2 (3⅜") red squares to 1 brown rectangle to form B/C Goose Chase Unit. Refer to *Block Diagram* to be sure seams are in correct direction. Repeat to make total of 4 Goose Chase Units.

3. Stitch 1 cream C triangle to long red side of each Goose Chase Unit to complete 4 Diagonal Bar Units.

4. Stitch 1 Diagonal Bar Unit each to opposite sides of center A/B unit.

5. Make 2 Triangle Units by stitching 1 cream B triangle to each short end of remaining Diagonal Bar Units as shown.

6. Stitch Triangle Units to opposite sides of long center bar unit to complete block.

Rail Fence Strip

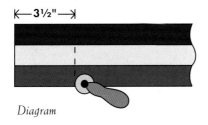

Strip Assembly Diagram

Finished Size: 3" x 42" strip

Materials
1½" x 24½" strips of 6 different dark fabrics
1½" x 24½" strips of 3 different light fabrics

Assembly
1. Join 2 dark and 1 light strips with light fabric in center. Repeat to make total of 3 strip sets. Press seam allowances toward dark fabrics.
2. From each strip set, cut 5 (3½") squares as shown in *Diagram.*

Diagram

3. Join 14 squares, alternating horizontal and vertical strips (see *Strip Assembly Diagram*). You will have 2 extra squares. If piecing quilt in vertical setting, join these extra squares and use them as spacer (see *Vertical Setting Diagram, Block* 30 on page 7.)

Rambler

Block Assembly Diagram   *Block Diagram*

Finished Size: 12" square

Materials
Scraps of white print, blue plaid, red plaid, dark
    plaid, and navy print

Cutting
From white print, cut:
- 1 (4¾") square (A).
- 4 (4¼") squares. Cut squares in quarters diagonally to make 16 triangles (C).

From blue plaid, cut:
- 2 (3⅞") squares. Cut squares in half diagonally to make 4 triangles (B).

From red plaid, cut:
- 2 (3⅞") squares. Cut squares in half diagonally to make 4 triangles (B).

From dark plaid, cut:
- 2 (3⅞") squares. Cut squares in half diagonally to make 4 triangles (B).

From navy print, cut:
- 1 (7¼") square. Cut in quarters diagonally to make 4 triangles (D).

Assembly

1. Join 2 white Cs to 1 blue plaid B to make Goose Chase Unit. Repeat to make total of 4 blue-and-white Goose Chase units and 4 red-and-white Goose Chase units.

2. Referring to *Block Assembly Diagram* on page 29, join 1 blue Goose Chase Unit to 1 red Goose Chase Unit. Add 1 dark plaid B to each blue plaid unit. Repeat to make total of 4 bar units.

3. Join 2 bar units to 2 sides of white A square to make center unit.

4. Join 1 navy D to sides of remaining bar units to make triangle units. Join triangle units to opposite sides of center unit to complete block.

Sawtooth Strip

Strip Assembly Diagram

Finished Size: 4" x 18" strip

Materials
1 (2⅞"-wide) strip tan print
11 assorted 2⅞" dark squares

Cutting
• Cut 11 (2⅞") squares from tan strip. Cut all squares in half diagonally to make 2 triangles each.

Assembly

1. Join triangle pairs to make total of 18 triangle-squares. If piecing quilt in vertical setting, join extra triangle pairs to make 4 additional triangle-squares.

2. Referring to *Strip Assembly Diagram*, make 2 rows of 9 triangle-squares each and join rows to make Sawtooth Strips. For vertical setting quilt top, join

remaining 4 triangle-squares in single row to use as spacer (see *Vertical Setting Diagram, Block* 37 on page 7.)

Log Cabin

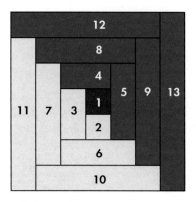

Block Assembly Diagram

Finished Size: 4 (7") squares

Materials
Scraps of 6 light fabrics
Scraps of 7 dark fabrics
4 (1½") squares of red solid fabric
Rotary cutter, mat, and ruler

Use definitely dark and definitely light fabrics and a few medium shades. Include a solid red for the center square of each block. The red center historically symbolizes the Log Cabin's hearth.

—Marianne

Assembly

1. Cut fabrics into 1½"-wide strips for logs. If using full-width fabric, cut crosswise strips. If using odd-sized scraps, cut strips on straight of grain, parallel to longest edge of fabric.

2. With right sides facing and raw edges aligned, place 1 center square on top of 1 light-colored strip. Stitch square to strip, sewing a few stitches beyond square. Lay another square on top of strip, approximately ¼" from first square; stitch second

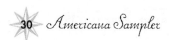

square to strip in same manner as above. Repeat to join all squares to strip.

3. Using rotary cutter and ruler, align ruler with raw edge of square (Photo A). Cut strip even with edges of center square. Press seam allowance away from center square, taking care not to distort shape of pieces. Repeat for all squares.

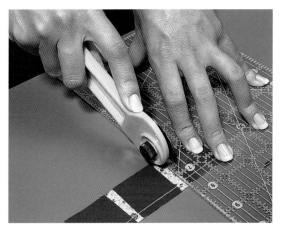

Photo A

4. With right sides facing and raw edges aligned, lay 2-square units on top of another light-colored strip (#3 in *Block Assembly Diagram*). Place 2-square units so that center squares (#1) precede light squares (#2) as you sew. Stitch 2-square units to strip as above. Cut strip even with edges of 2-square units to form 3-piece units (Photo B). Press seam allowances away from center squares.

Photo B

5. Place 3-piece units atop 1 dark strip so that previously sewn log of each unit (#3) is sewn last. Stitch units to dark strip. Cut strip even with units as shown in Photo C to form 4-piece unit. Press seam allowances away from center squares.

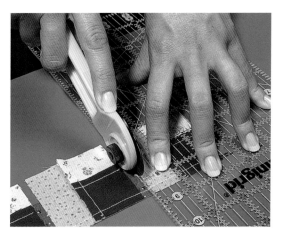

Photo C

6. In same manner, stitch 4-piece units to dark strip (#5). Continue in this manner, using light strips for 1 diagonal half and dark strips for other half, until 4 Log Cabin Blocks are complete. Remember to position units correctly on top of strips; last log added should always be closest to you as you sew.

7. Check that all blocks are approximately same size. If using 1½"-wide cut strips and blocks were stitched according to *Block Assembly Diagram* and photos, finished blocks should each measure 7½" square with seam allowances.

Be sure your seam allowance is exactly ¼". If seams are too deep, your block will be too small.

—Marianne

Floral Wreath

Block Diagram

Finished Size: 15" square

Materials

1 (15½") square tan print
¼ yard green print
Scraps of red solid, red print, pink print, and
    yellow print
Template plastic

Cutting

Make templates for patterns A, B, C, D, E, and F.
See patterns on page 46. Add ³⁄₁₆" seam allowance
when cutting out appliqués.

From green print, cut:
• 4 (1" x 7") bias strips for wreath.
• 12 green print leaves (A).

From red solid, cut:
• 4 tulip tips (B).
• 1 outer posy (D).

From red print, cut:
• 4 tulips (C).

From pink print, cut:
• 1 inner posy (E).

From yellow print, cut:
• 1 center (F).

Assembly

1. Center and mark pattern placement lines from
page 46 on background fabric, using your favorite
method. Mark only inner curve of bias strips.
2. Fold bias strips in thirds lengthwise; press.
Appliqué bias stem onto tan background, starting

with inner edge. Leave about ¼" of stem extend-
ing into tulip area.
3. Prepare appliqués and appliqué in following
order: leaves (A), tulip tips (B), tulips (C), outer
posy (D), inner posy (E), and center (F). Trim fabric from back of appliqués to reduce bulk.

North Carolina Lily

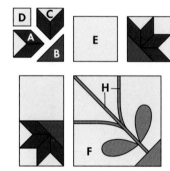

Block Assembly Diagram

Block Diagram

Finished Size: 12½" square

Materials

Scraps of red and dark green prints
¼ yard green print
¼ yard white-on-white print
Template plastic

Cutting

Make templates for patterns A and G. See patterns
on page 45. Use large needle to poke holes in
Template A at corner dots. Add ³⁄₁₆" seam
allowance when cutting out leaf appliqués.

From red print, cut:
- 12 As, using template. Mark fabric pieces through holes in template.

From dark green print, cut:
- 2 (3⅜") squares. Cut squares in half diagonally to make 4 B lily triangles.

From green print, cut:
- 1 (3⅜") square. Cut square in half diagonally to make 2 B base triangles. (You will have 1 extra.)
- 2 G leaves, using template.
- Approximately 24" of ¾"-wide bias. Fold in thirds to make ¼"-wide finished bias for stems (H).

From white-on-white print, cut:
- 2 (3¾") squares. Cut squares in quarters diagonally to make 8 Cs. (You will have 2 extra.)
- 3 (2¼") squares (D).
- 2 (4½" x 4¾") rectangles (E).
- 1 (8¾") square (F).

Assembly

1. Referring to *Diagram*, join 4 As to make lily. Add 1 dark green B to bottom. Set in 2 C triangles and 1 D square to complete lily unit. Repeat to make total of 3 units.

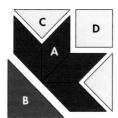

Diagram

2. Referring to *Block Assembly Diagram*, appliqué 3 H stems and 2 G leaves to F. Join 1 lily unit to 1 E. Join to left side of F as shown. Join 2 lily units to remaining E rectangle. Join to top of E/F unit.
3. Appliqué green B triangle to corner of F. Trim excess F from back of block. Press block.

Criss-Cross

Block Assembly Diagram

Block Diagram

Finished Size: 6" square

Materials
Scraps of red, black, and white prints

Cutting

From red print, cut:
- 1 (3¼") square. Cut in quarters diagonally to make 4 triangles (B).

From black print, cut:
- 1 (2"-wide) strip. Cut 4 (2" x 3⅜") rectangles (A).

From white, cut:
- 1 (5¼") square. Cut in quarters diagonally to make 4 triangles (C).

Assembly

1. Join 1 red triangle B to short end of 1 black rectangle A. Repeat to make total of 4 units.
2. Join 1 white triangle C to each A/B unit (*Diagram*).

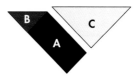

Diagram

3. Referring to *Block Assembly Diagram*, join the 4 triangle units to complete block.

Schoolhouse

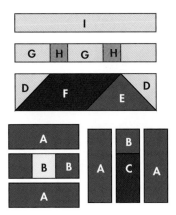

Block Assembly Diagram

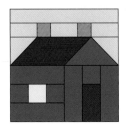

Block Diagram

Finished Size: 6" square

Materials

Scraps of blue stripe, cream print, white print, plaid, black-and-white check, and red print

Cutting

From blue stripe, cut:
- 4 (1½" x 3½") rectangles (A).
- 3 (1½") squares for house (B).
- 1 (2" x 3½") rectangle for house peak (E).

From cream print, cut:
- 2 (2") squares (D).
- 3 (1¼" x 2") rectangles (G).
- 1 (1¼" x 6½") rectangle for sky (I).

From white print, cut:
- 1 (1½") square for window (B).

From plaid, cut:
- 1 (1½" x 2½") rectangle for door (C).

From black-and-white check, cut:
- 2 (1¼") squares for chimneys (H).

From red print, cut:
- 1 (2" x 5") rectangle for roof (F).

Assembly

1. Referring to *Block Assembly Diagram*, stitch 1 blue stripe B to top of door C. Add 1 A rectangle to each side.

2. Stitch 1 blue stripe B to opposite sides of window B. Add 1 A rectangle to top and bottom. Join window unit to door unit.

3. Referring to *Diagram* and using diagonal-seams method (see page 21), join house peak E to roof F. Place 1 sky D square atop both ends of E/F unit and stitch, using diagonal seams. Stitch roof row to top of house.

4. Join sky G rectangles and H chimney squares. Stitch to top of roof row.

5. Stitch sky I to top of chimney row.

Diagram

Cross and Crown

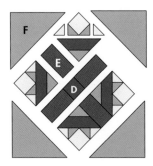

Block Assembly Diagram

Block Diagram

Finished Size: 14" square

Materials

¼ yard tan-and-black print
⅛ yard or 1 (2½" x 21") piece brown stripe
1 (6" x 11") piece blue-and-red paisley
⅛ yard or 1 (3¼" x 13") piece tan-and-white print
⅛ yard or 1 (3¼" x 18") piece black-and-white miniprint

Cutting

From tan-and-black print, cut:
- 2 (7⅞") squares. Cut squares in half diagonally to make 4 triangles (F).

From brown stripe, cut:
- 1 (2½"-wide) strip. Cut strip into 4 (2½" x 4½") rectangles (E).

From blue-and-red paisley, cut:
- 2 (4⅞") squares. Cut squares in half diagonally (A).
- 1 (2½") square (D).

From tan-and-white print, cut:
- 4 (2½") squares (B).
- 2 (3¼") squares. Cut squares in quarters diagonally to make 8 quarter-square triangles (C).

From black-and-white miniprint, cut:
- 4 (2½") squares (D).
- 2 (3¼") squares. Cut squares in quarters diagonally to make 8 quarter-square triangles (C).

Assembly

1. Referring to *Diagram 1* and using diagonal-seams method (see page 21), add 2½" tan-and-white square to blue-and-red paisley triangle. Repeat to make total of 4 units.

2. Join 1 tan/white C to 1 black/white C triangle; make 4 units with tan/white on right and 4 units with tan/white on left.

3. Join 1 C unit to 2 sides of black/white D square as shown in *Diagram 2*. Join A/B unit to C/D unit to complete crown unit (*Diagram 3*). Repeat to make total of 4 crown units.

Diagram 1

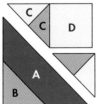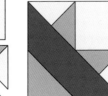

Diagram 2   *Diagram 3*

4. Referring to *Block Assembly Diagram*, join brown E to opposite sides of blue D. Join 1 crown unit to each side of remaining Es. Join units to complete center of block.

5. Add outer triangles F to complete block. Press.

Goose Chase Strip

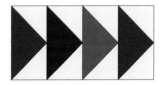

Strip Diagram

Finished Size: 2 (6" x 12") strips

Materials

1 (3½" x 6½") rectangle from each of 8 fabrics
16 (3½") squares cream fabric

Assembly

1. Use diagonal-seams method (see page 21) to stitch 1 cream square to each end of 1 scrap rectangle as shown in *Diagrams*. Repeat to make 8 Goose Chase Units.

2. Referring to *Strip Diagram*, join 4 Goose Chase Units to make 1 strip. Repeat to make total of 2 strips.

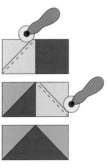

Diagrams

Bear's Paw

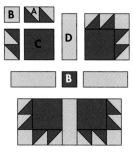

Block Assembly Diagram   Block Diagram

Finished Size: 14" square

Materials
Scraps blue and white-and-blue prints

Cutting

From blue print, cut:
- 8 (2⅞") squares. Cut squares in half diagonally to make 16 As.
- 1 (2½") square (B).
- 4 (4½") squares (C).

From white-and-blue print, cut:
- 8 (2⅞") squares. Cut squares in half diagonally to make 16 As.
- 4 (2½") squares (B).
- 4 (2½" x 6½") rectangles (D).

Assembly

1. Join 1 blue A to 1 white A along long sides (*Diagram 1*). Repeat to make total of 16 triangle-squares.

2. Referring to *Diagram 2*, join 2 A units as shown; join to 1 side of C. Join 2 A units to 1 white B square. Join to top of A/C unit to make paw unit. Repeat to make total of 4 paw units.

Diagram 1

Diagram 2

3. Lay out remaining pieces as shown in *Block Assembly Diagram*. Join 2 paw units to a D rectangle to make top row. Repeat with remaining paw units for bottom row. Join 1 D rectangle to opposite sides of blue B square for middle row.

4. Join rows to complete block. Press.

Hawaiian Breadfruit

Block Diagram

Finished Size: 15" square

Materials
1 (17") square solid cream for background
1 (16") square dark print for motif
Freezer paper

Assembly

1. Trace quarter pattern on page 47 onto a 7" square of freezer paper. Cut out.

2. Fold dark print into fourths. Press pattern, shiny side down, onto top layer, aligning broken lines of pattern with fabric folds. Pin layers together to prevent shifting. Cut out along solid lines of pattern through all layers, adding ⅛" seam allowance. Remove pattern; press fabric.

3. Fold cream background into fourths and lightly press to form guidelines. Pin appliqué in place on background; baste and remove pins. Appliqué in place, turning under seam allowance with your needle as you stitch.

4. Trim background to 15½" square.

·Heart Basket·

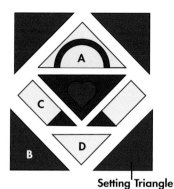

Setting Triangle

Block Assembly Diagram

Block Diagram

Finished Size: 12½" square

Materials

Scraps of blue print for basket, cream print for
background, and red print for setting triangles
Plastic-coated freezer paper
Paper-backed fusible web, embroidery floss and
needle (optional)

Cutting

From blue print, cut:

- 1 (7⅝") square; cut square in half diagonally
  to make 2 triangles A. (One is extra.)
- 1 (3⅛") square; cut square in half diagonally to
  make 2 triangles B.
- 1 (1¼" x 9") bias strip for handle.

From cream print, cut:

- 1 (7⅝") square; cut square in half diagonally to
  make 2 triangles A. (One is extra.)
- 2 (2¾" x 5") rectangles C.
- 1 (5⅜") square; cut square in half diagonally
  to make 2 triangles D. (One is extra.)

From red print, cut:

- 1 heart E. (See page 48 for pattern. See tip box
  on page 39 to choose method of appliqué before
  cutting heart.)
- 2 (7½") squares. Cut squares in half diagonally to
  make 4 setting triangles.

*The setting triangles are slightly oversize, but you'll
square up the block later.*

—Liz

Assembly

1. Referring to *Basket Piecing Diagram*, piece bottom
basket section of block.

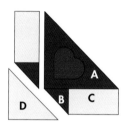

Basket Piecing Diagram

Adding Handle

2. To make handle placement guide, cut 7⅝"
square from freezer paper; cut square in half diagonally to make triangle A pattern. (Discard extra
triangle pattern.) Fold template in half, with shiny
sides facing, and sketch inner curve of handle on
uncoated (dull) side of paper (Photo A).

Photo A

3. To complete handle curve, turn template over and trace drawn line on other half. Unfold template and check to be sure curve fits basket section of block (Photo B). Cut along line to make handle placement guide. Discard outer portion of paper.

Photo B

4. Fold cream triangle A in half and press lightly to mark center guideline. Place shiny side of template against right side of fabric, aligning template fold with fabric center guideline and making sure straight edge of pattern is ¼" from raw edge of fabric. Use wool setting and no steam to lightly press handle placement guide to fabric triangle (Photo C).

Photo C

5. With wrong sides facing, fold bias strip in thirds lengthwise and steam-press (Photo D). Folded bias strip will be approximately ⅜" wide.

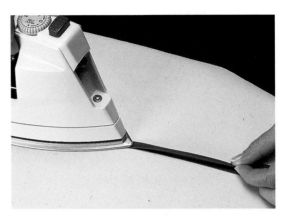

Photo D

6. Baste bottom (inner) edge of folded strip along edge of handle placement guide (Photo E), allowing ends of strip to extend beyond raw edges of fabric triangle. Peel away paper guide. (Do not appliqué handle yet.)

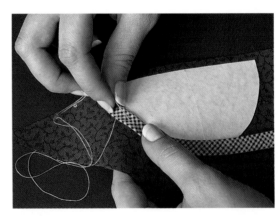

Photo E

7. Join handle section to basket section along straight edges to complete block center.

8. Appliqué edges of handle to block, stitching inner curve first and then outer curve. Turn block over and trim excess ends of handle even with seam allowances.

Appliquéing Heart

9. Fold basket in half diagonally and finger-press to mark center guideline for heart. Center and pin heart so that bottom point of heart is 1½" from bottom point of pieced basket. Appliqué heart to basket using one of the following methods.

10. When appliqué is completed, turn block to back, separate heart fabric from basket fabric, and cut small slit in basket fabric only. Trim basket fabric from behind heart appliqué, leaving ⅛" seam allowance. Remove freezer paper, using tweezers if needed.

Finishing Block

11. Join 2 setting triangles to opposite sides of block (*Block Assembly Diagram* on page 37); press. Join remaining triangles to opposite sides of block; press. Triangles will extend over edges of basket block. Using large rotary-cutting square ruler, trim block to 13" square.

Methods of Appliqué

Method 1

Cut out heart, adding ¼" seam allowance. Turn under edges and baste. Pin heart in position on basket and appliqué as desired. (If you choose to use blanket stitches, place stitches approximately ⅛" apart and refer to *Blanket-Stitch Diagram* below.)

Blanket-Stitch Diagram

Method 2

Cut out heart, adding ⅛" seam allowance and needle-turn appliqué heart to basket.

Method 3

Iron paper-backed fusible web to wrong side of heart fabric. Cut out heart along marked line. Fuse heart to basket. Using 2 strands of embroidery floss, blanket-stitch heart to basket, spacing stitches about ¼" apart (see *Blanket-Stitch Diagram*).

Method 4

Trace heart pattern onto uncoated (dull) side of freezer paper and cut. Pin freezer paper pattern, shiny side up, to fabric. Cut out heart, adding ¼" seam allowance. Using only the tip of dry iron, press seam allowance to shiny side of freezer paper. Appliqué as desired.

Quilt Assembly

Once you have made all of your blocks for your sampler, the real fun begins—deciding how to set the blocks for your quilt. We have given you two setting options, a vertical layout and a horizontal layout, on pages 6 and 7. If you choose to use one of our block arrangements, remember that you can switch around blocks that are the same size to personalize your quilt. For example, the quilt contains several 12"-square blocks, Grandmother's Fan, Windblown Square, Royal Cross, Ohio Star, Wheels, Sawtooth Star, Gentleman's Fancy, LeMoyne Star, Dresden Plate, and Rambler. Schoolhouse, Criss-Cross, and Goose Chase Strip also combine to make a 12" unit. You can interchange the positions fo any of these 12"-square units within your quilt.

Join blocks together into larger rectangular or square units as shown in the setting diagrams. Build out from the largest block—the Lone Star— and add either the row of Log Cabin Blocks or the Cross and Crown and Bear's Paw row to the side of the Lone Star. You will now have the large unit that is equal in size to the next unit that you will add. Continue in this manner until all units are joined. We chose not to add borders to our quilts in keeping with the Nineteenth-century sampler tradition. However, feel free to add borders to your quilt to make it larger if you wish. If you choose to add borders, you will probably need about 3 yards of border fabric for lengthwise cut borders. Cut borders for the longest sides first and add them to the quilt top. Then cut and add borders for the shorter sides.

Finishing Materials

6 yards backing fabric
1 yard binding fabric
Full-size quilt batting (81" x 96")

1. Divide backing fabric into 2 (3-yard) pieces. Cut 1 piece in half lengthwise. Join 1 half piece to each side of full-width piece. Press seam allowances open to reduce bulk when quilting.
2. Mark quilting designs as desired. Layer quilt top, batting, and backing; baste. Quilt as desired.
3. From binding fabric, cut approximately 350" of 2¼"-wide binding. (If you added borders to your quilt, you will need to cut additional binding.) Make French-fold binding by folding binding strip in half, with wrong sides facing, so that binding is 1⅛" wide. Align raw edges of binding with raw edge of quilt top and sew through all layers with ¼"-wide seam, mitering corners of binding. Trim edges of quilt. Bring folded edge of binding to back of quilt and blindstitch in place.

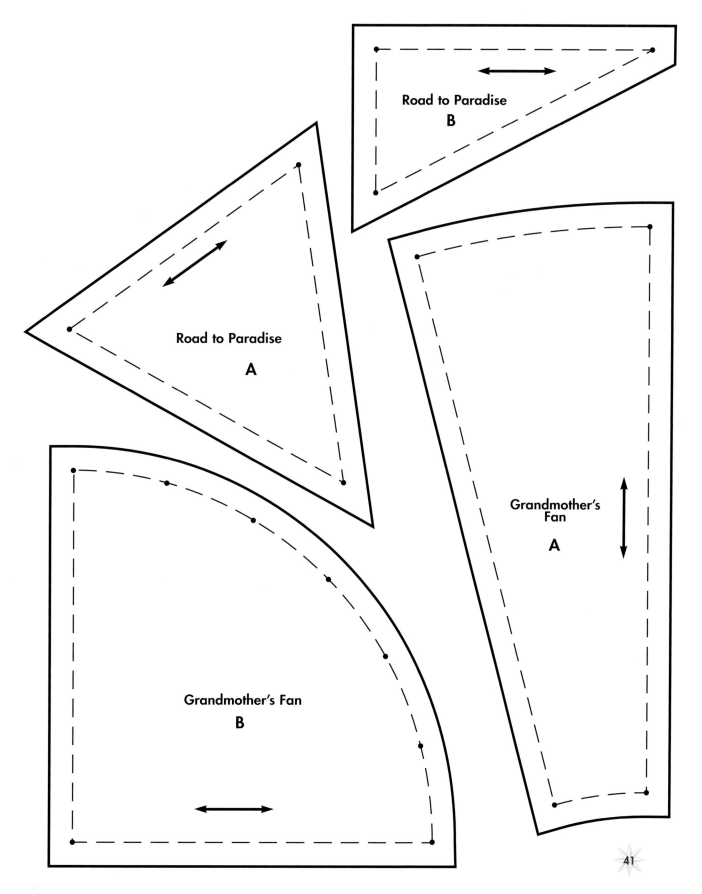

Road to Paradise
B

Road to Paradise
A

Grandmother's
Fan
A

Grandmother's Fan
B

Dotted lines indicate where patterns overlap.

Country Angel

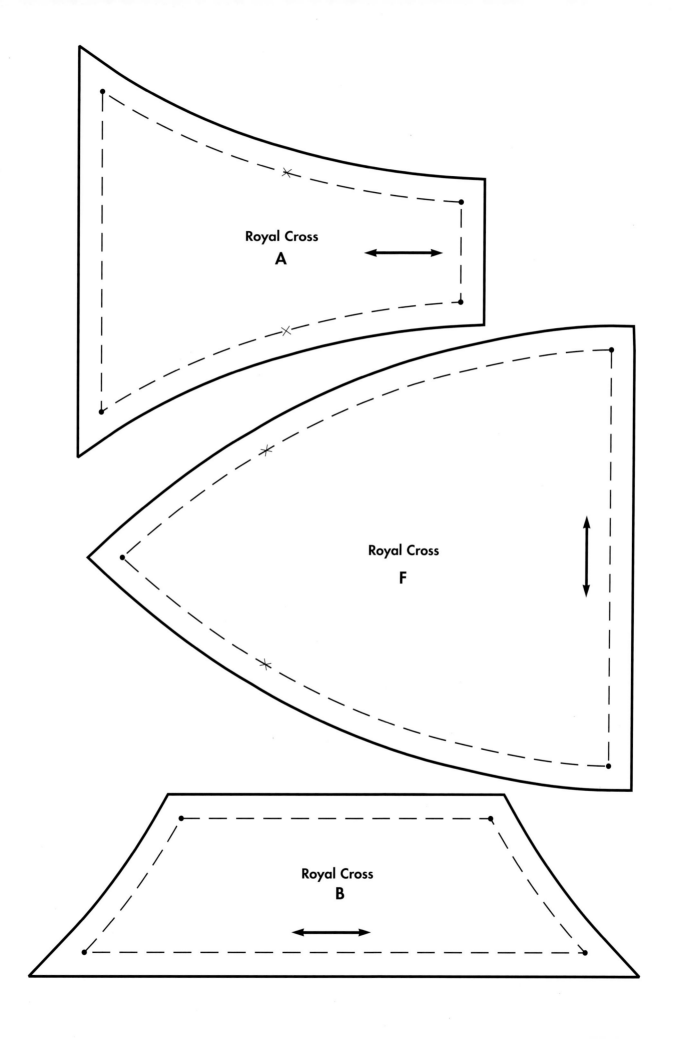

Royal Cross
A

Royal Cross
F

Royal Cross
B

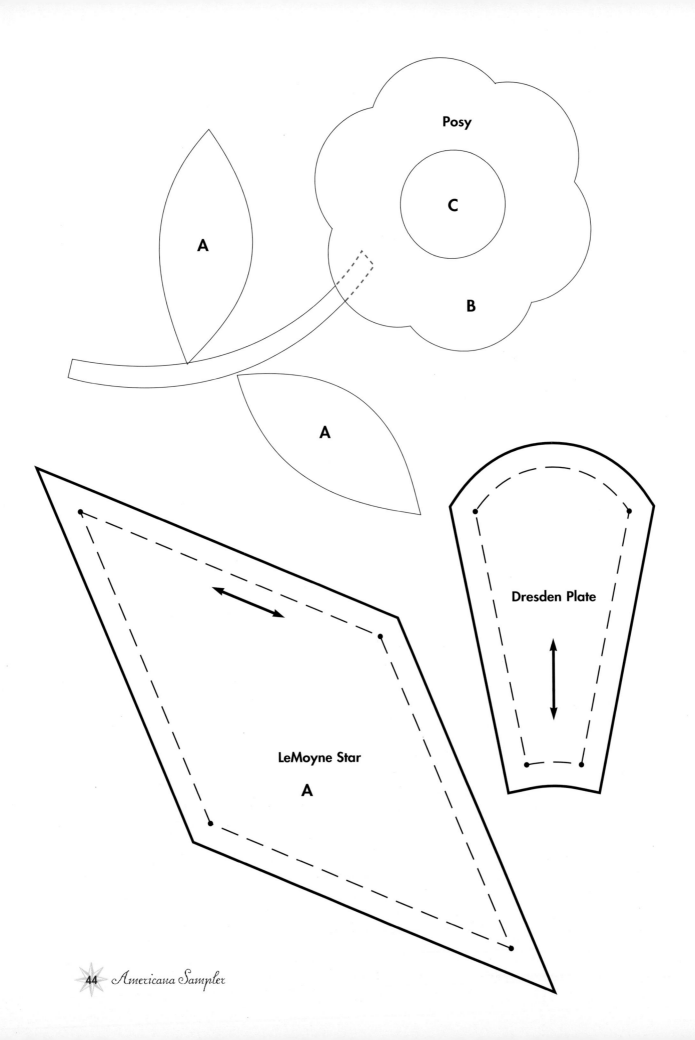

Posy

C

B

A

A

LeMoyne Star

A

Dresden Plate

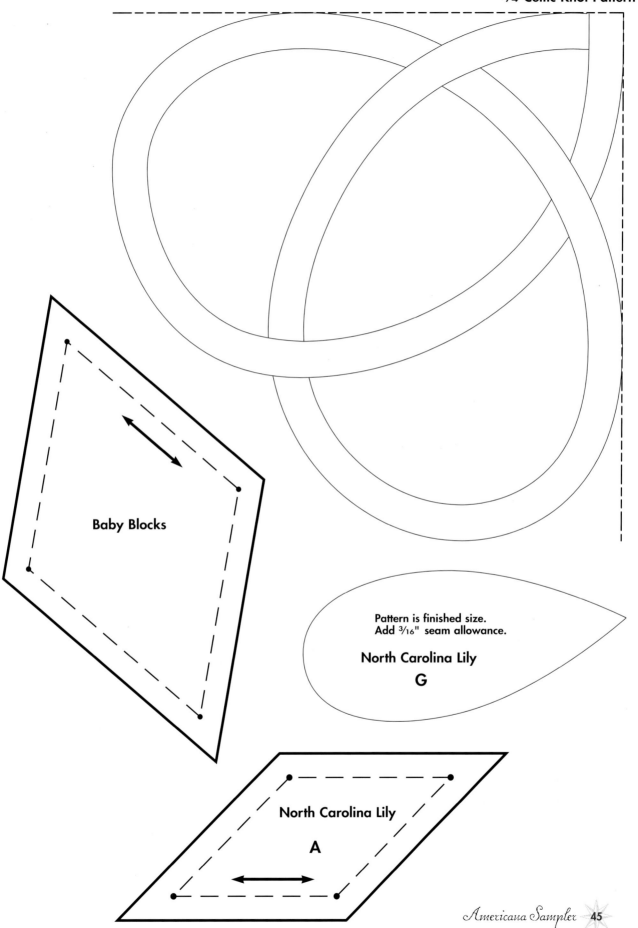

Baby Blocks

Pattern is finished size.
Add ³⁄₁₆" seam allowance.

North Carolina Lily
G

North Carolina Lily

A

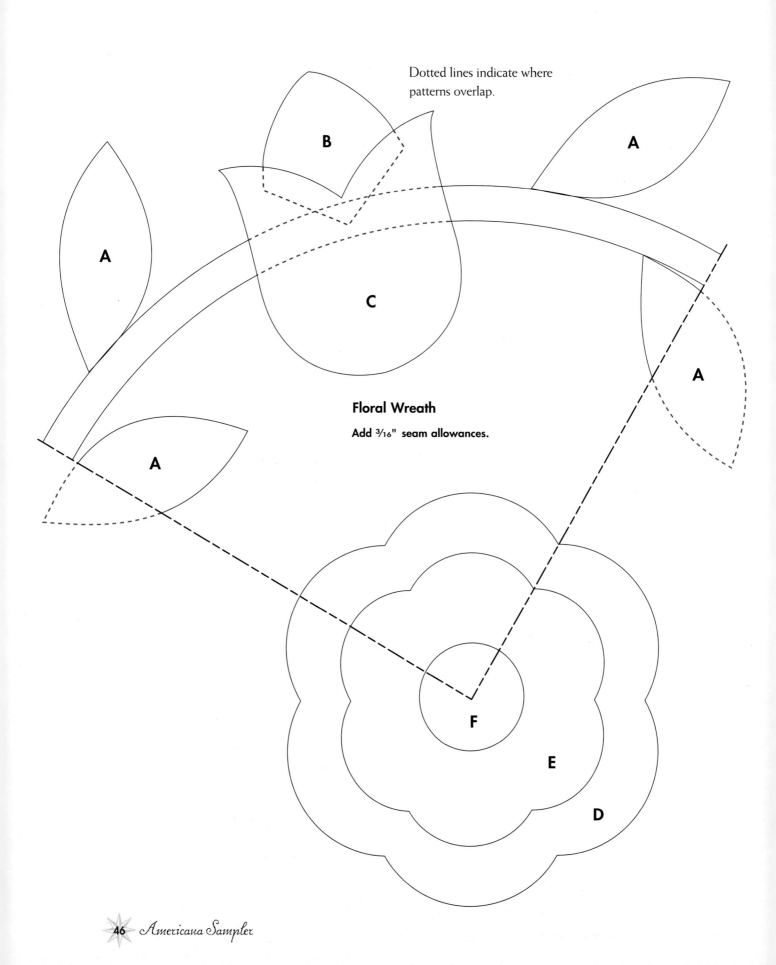

Dotted lines indicate where patterns overlap.

B

A

A

C

A

A

Floral Wreath

Add 3/16" seam allowances.

F

E

D

¼ Hawaiian Breadfruit Pattern

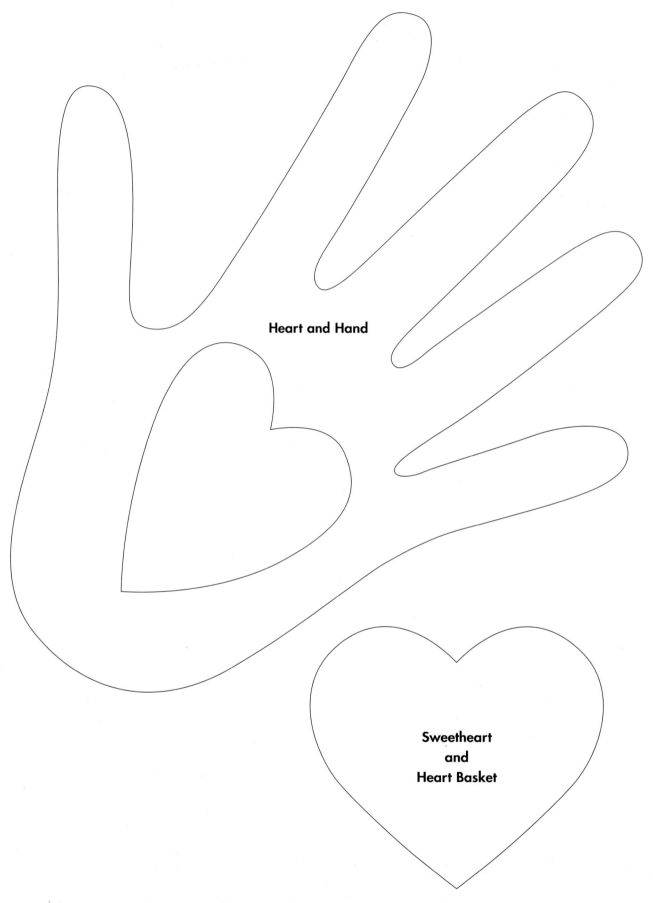

Heart and Hand

**Sweetheart
and
Heart Basket**